animal babies
on the farm

KINGFISHER

Kingfisher Publications Plc
New Penderel House
283–288 High Holborn
London WC1V 7HZ
www.kingfisherpub.com

First published by Kingfisher Publications Plc 2005
10 9 8 7 6 5 4 3 2 1
1TR/1204/TWP/SGCH(SGCH)/150STORA/C

Copyright © Kingfisher Publications Plc 2005

A CIP catalogue record for this book is available from the British Library.

ISBN–13: 978 0 7534 1076 9
ISBN–10: 0 7534 1076 1

Author and Editor: Vicky Weber
Designer: Joanne Brown
Picture Manager: Cee Weston-Baker
Picture Researcher: Rachael Swann
DTP Co-ordinator: Carsten Lorenz
Senior Production Controller: Lindsey Scott

Printed in Singapore

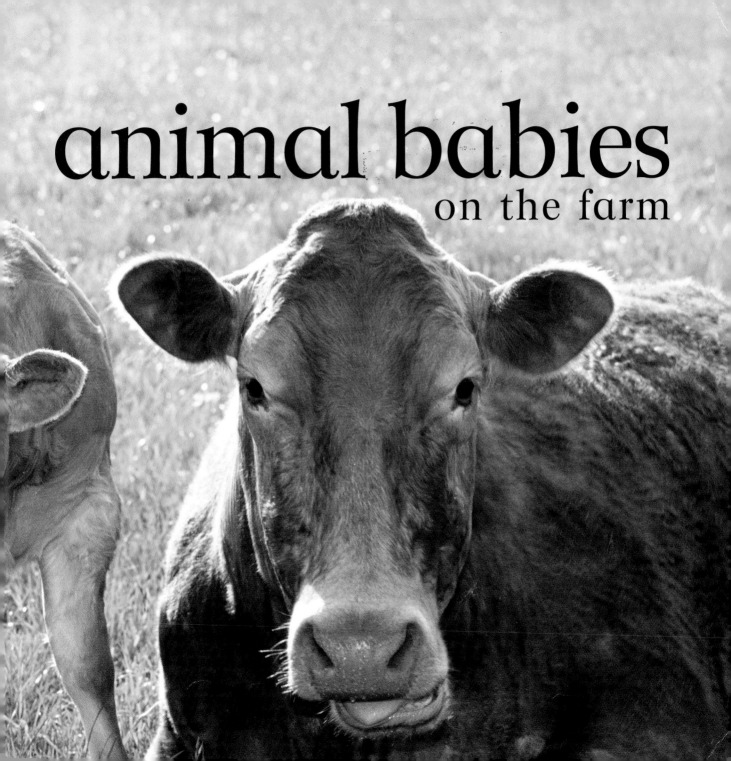

animal babies

on the farm

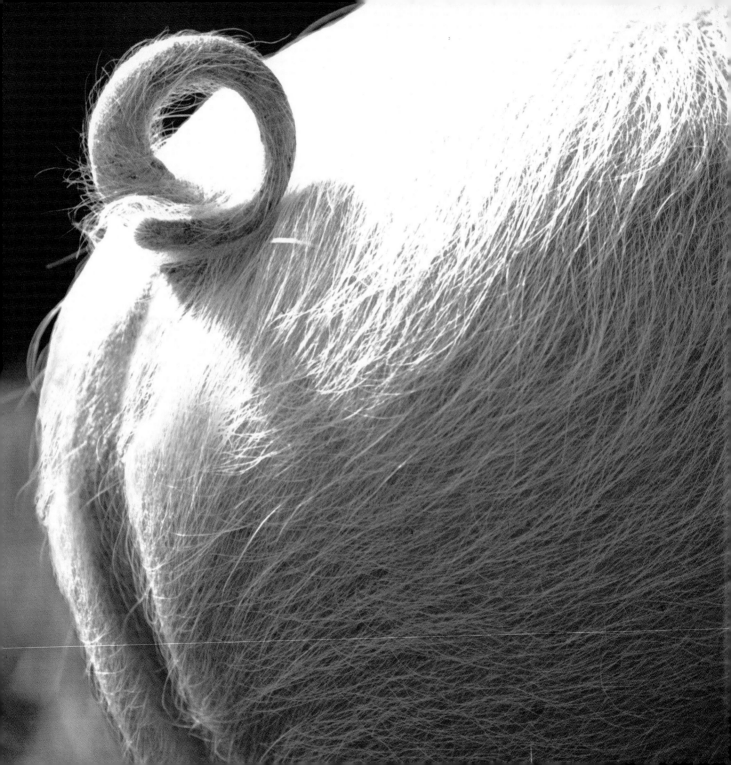

I have a **curly** tail
and **pink** skin. In very
hot sun, my **skin** can get
burnt – just like **yours**!

Who is my mummy?

My **mummy** is a pig
and I am her **piglet**.

We have big **floppy** ears
and a **snuffling** snout.
We can **hear** and
smell really well.

I have a long tail and a flowing mane. If you brush these, the hair becomes soft and shiny.

Who is my mummy?

My **mummy** is a horse and I am her **foal**.

We have **strong** legs and **hard** hooves. This means we can gallop very **fast**.

I have fluffy yellow feathers and a very sharp beak. I use my beak to peck at grain.

Who is my mummy?

My mummy is a chicken and I am her chick.

We use our clawed feet to scratch the hard ground in the farmyard.

I love skipping around in the crisp spring air and eating the fresh green grass.

Who is my mummy?

My mummy is a sheep and I am her lamb.

When our coat grows long, it is cut off and our fur is made into wool.

I like **drinking** mummy's **creamy** milk just as much as you do. I **enjoy** eating **grass** as well.

Who is my mummy?

My mummy
is a cow and
I am her calf.

We spend our
days grazing
lazily in the
grassy field.

My neck will become longer and longer as I grow up. When I am upset, I stretch my neck and honk noisily.

Who is my mummy?

My mummy is a goose and I am her gosling.

We use our webbed feet to paddle quickly in the water as we search for tasty pond plants to eat.

I have a thick, furry coat. This keeps me snug when it is cold. When I am older, I will grow a beard.

Who is my mummy?

My **mummy** is a goat and I am her **kid**.

We like **eating!** We **munch** grass in the pasture. In fact, we eat **anything** we can find. Yum yum.

Note

All of the animals shown in this book can be tamed if they are kept on farms. However, no animal should be approached without an adult's permission, and never go near when they are feeding. Many of these animals can also live in the wild. If you see them in the open countryside, do not get too close as they may become frightened and attack you – always keep a safe distance.

Acknowledgements

The publisher would like to thank the following for permission to reproduce their material. Every care has been taken to trace copyright holders. However, if there have been unintentional omissions or failure to trace copyright holders, we apologise and will, if informed, endeavour to make corrections in any future edition.

Cover: Getty Images; Half title: Getty Images; Title page: Agripicture Images/Alamy; Pig 1: bildagentur-online.com/ th-foto/ Alamy; Pig 2: John Daniels/ardea.com; Horse 1: Aiden Clayton/Alamy; Horse 2: FLPA/Minden Pictures/M Iwago; Chicken 1: Getty Images; Chicken 2: John Daniels/ ardea.com; Sheep 1: Getty Images; Sheep 2: Agripicture Images/Alamy; Cow 1: Agripicture Images/ Peter Dean; Cow 2: Agripicture Images/Alamy; Goose 1: ImageState/Alamy; Goose 2: Hans Reinhard/Bruce Coleman Ltd; Goat 1: Finnbarr Webster/Alamy; Goat 2: Craig Lovell/Corbis.